Balloon Trail

Trace the sleeping lines to complete the pattern on the balloons. Color the balloons.

Spider Web

Trace the standing lines and help the spiders climb down the wall.

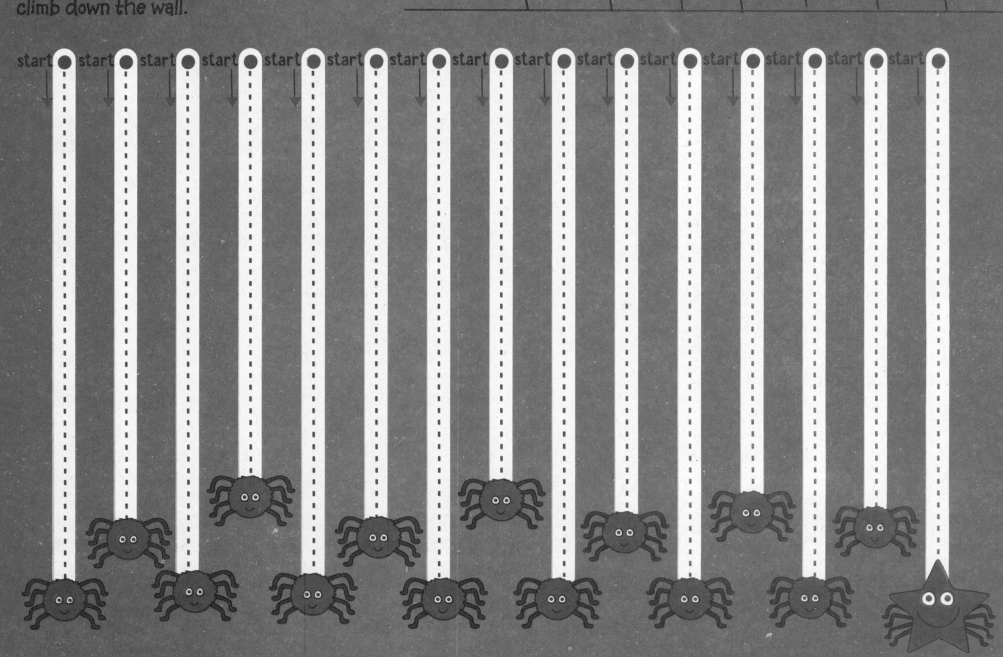

Leaf Patterns

Trace the slanted lines inside the leaves. Color the leaves brightly.

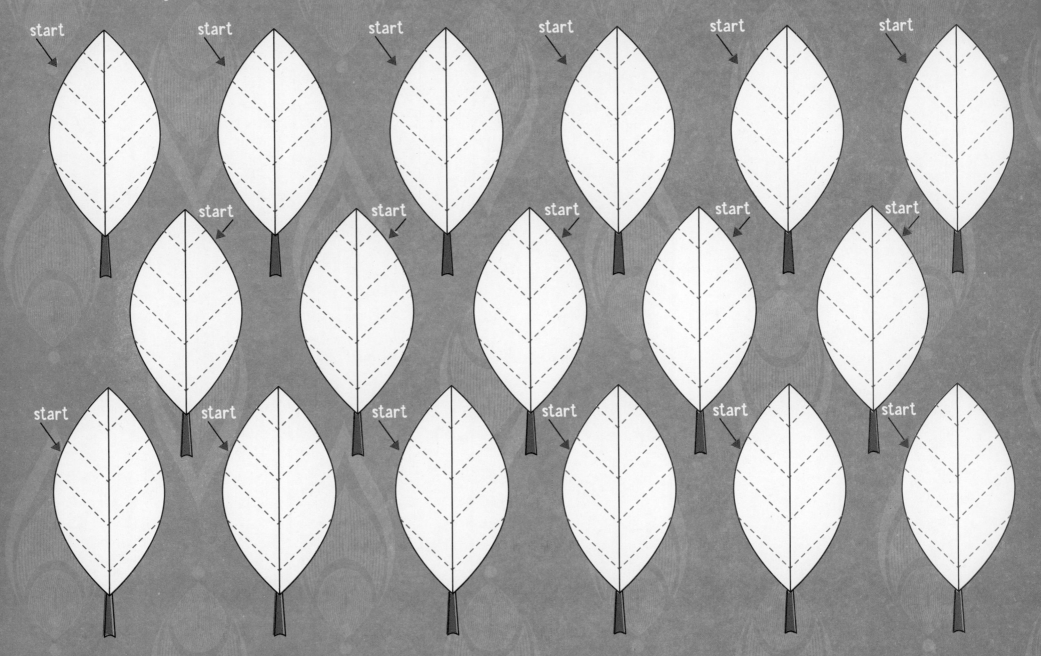

Coniferous Forest

Trace the zig-zag lines to complete the trees in the forest. Don't forget to color the trees.

start

start

start

start

start

Leaping Frogs

Trace the curved lines and help the frogs reach the lily pads.

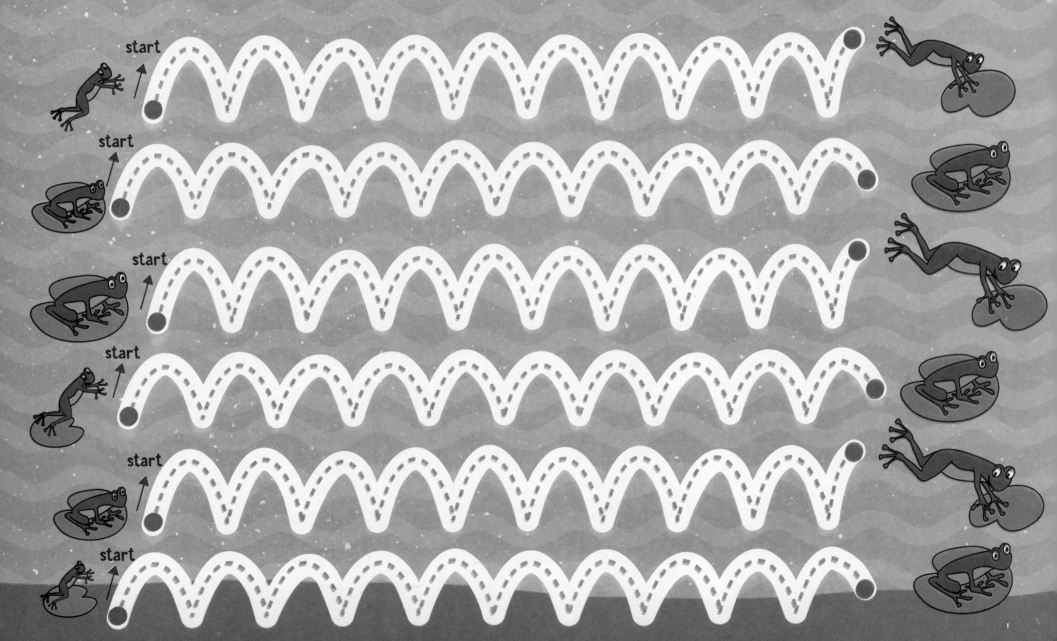

Whale Family

Trace the curved lines and unite the baby whales with their mothers.

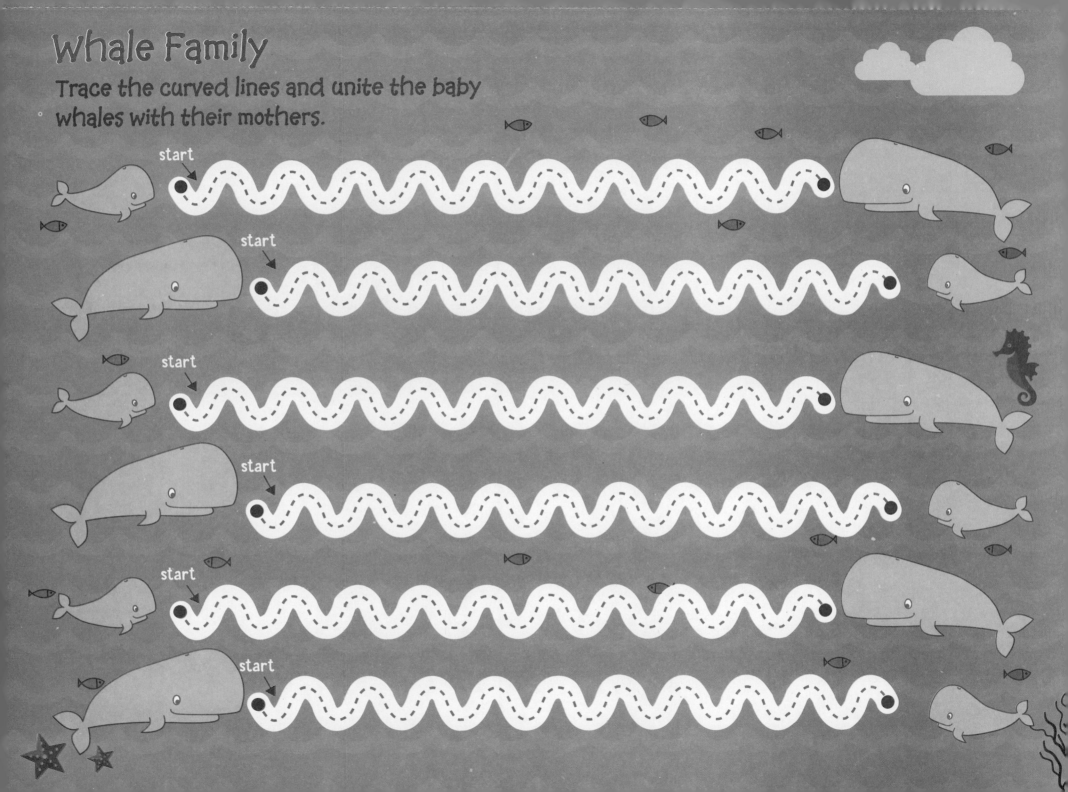

start

start

start

start

start

start

Telephone Ring

Trace the loops to pick up the telephone.

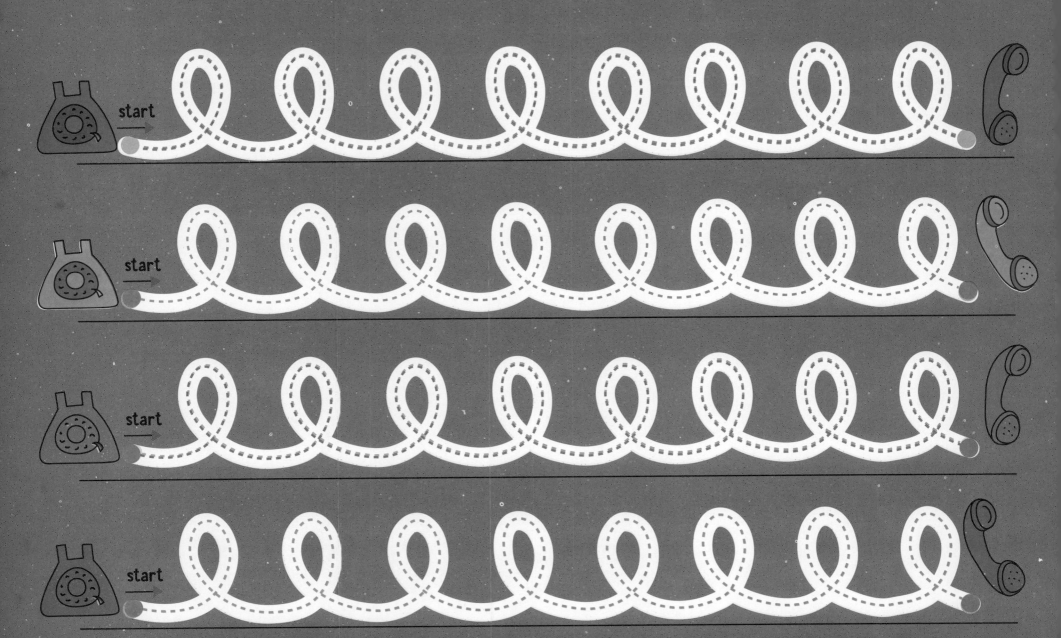

Garden Insects

Trace the multiple line patterns and help the insects reach their friends in the garden.

start

start

start

start

start

Trace the patterns and help the tractors reach the farm.

start

start

start

start

Dino World

Trace the line patterns and help the dinosaurs escape the volcanoes.

start

start

start

start

start

Beach Fun

Complete the beach scene by tracing the multiple patterns.

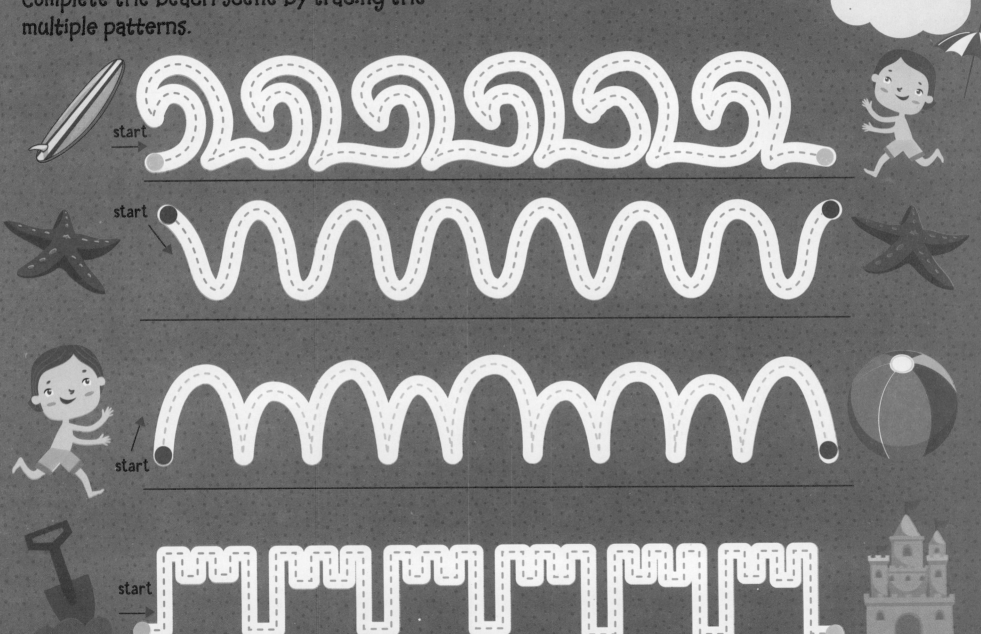

start

start

start

start

Grape Vineyard

Trace the circles to draw the grapes. Color the grapes brightly.

Tortoise Race

Trace the semicircles and complete the picture.
Color the tortoises brightly.

Birthday Presents

Trace the lines to complete the square presents.
Don't forget to color the presents.

Postal Service

Trace the rectangles and slanted lines to draw the envelopes. Color the envelopes brightly.

start

start

start

start

start

start

start

start

start

Racing Sailboats

Trace the triangles to draw the sails
of the boats racing in the ocean.
Color the sails brightly.

start

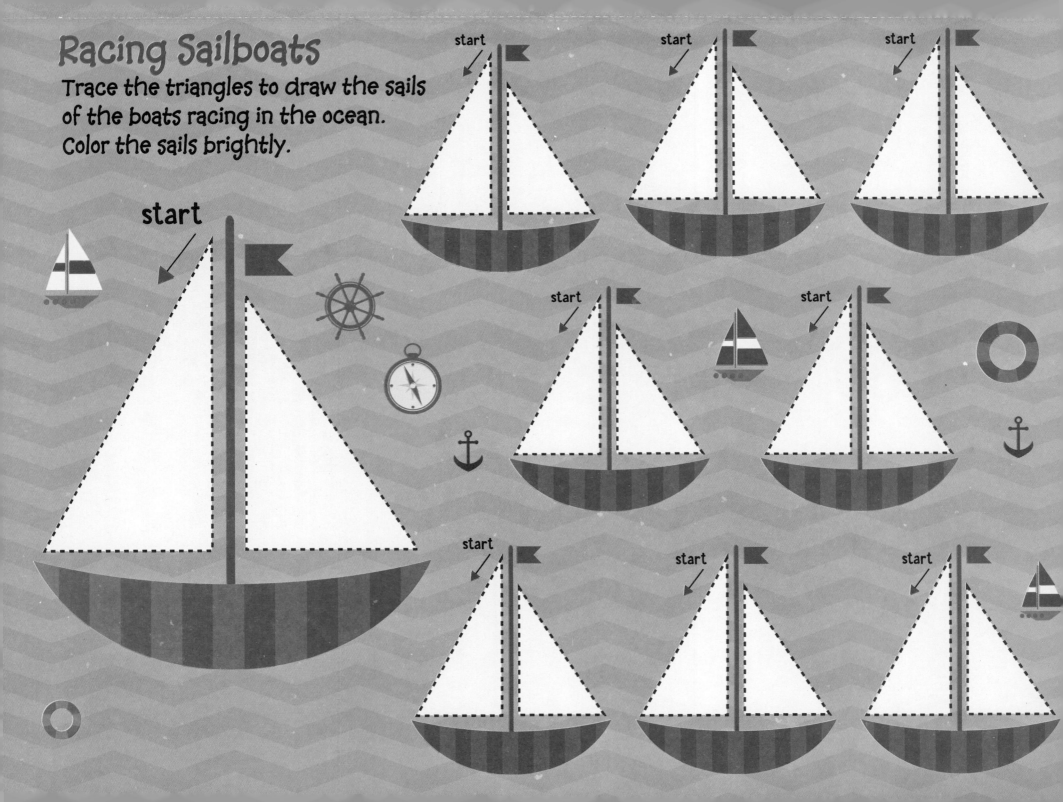

Animal Express

Trace the lines and complete the train. Can you guess all the shapes in the train?

City Street

Trace the lines and complete the buildings on the street. Don't forget to color the windows.

Strawberry Bloom

Trace the oval seeds inside the strawberries.
Color the strawberries brightly.

Floating Hearts

Trace the heart-shaped patterns and complete the picture. Don't forget to color the hearts.

start

start

start

start

start

start

start

start

start

start

start

start

Starry Night

Trace the patterns and draw the stars in the night sky.

Frozen Treat

Trace the patterns to complete the picture.
Color the ice cream cones brightly.

Raindrops

Trace the rain drops and complete the picture.
Color the drops.

Trace the patterns on the Easter eggs.
Color the Easter eggs brightly.

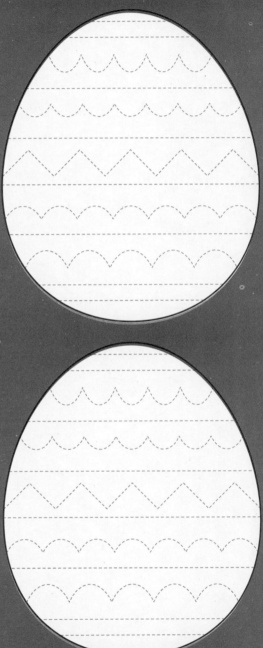

Candy Treat

Trace the spiral lines to draw the lollipops. Color the lollipops brightly.

start

start

start

start

start

start

start

start

start

start

start

Bee Trail

Trace the spiral lines to help the bees reach the flowers.

start

start

start

start

start

start

start

start

Happy Jellyfish

Trace the wavy lines and complete the picture.

Pumpkin Patch

Trace the lines to draw the pumpkins. Color the pumpkins.

Butterfly Park

Trace the lines to draw the butterflies. Color the butterflies brightly.

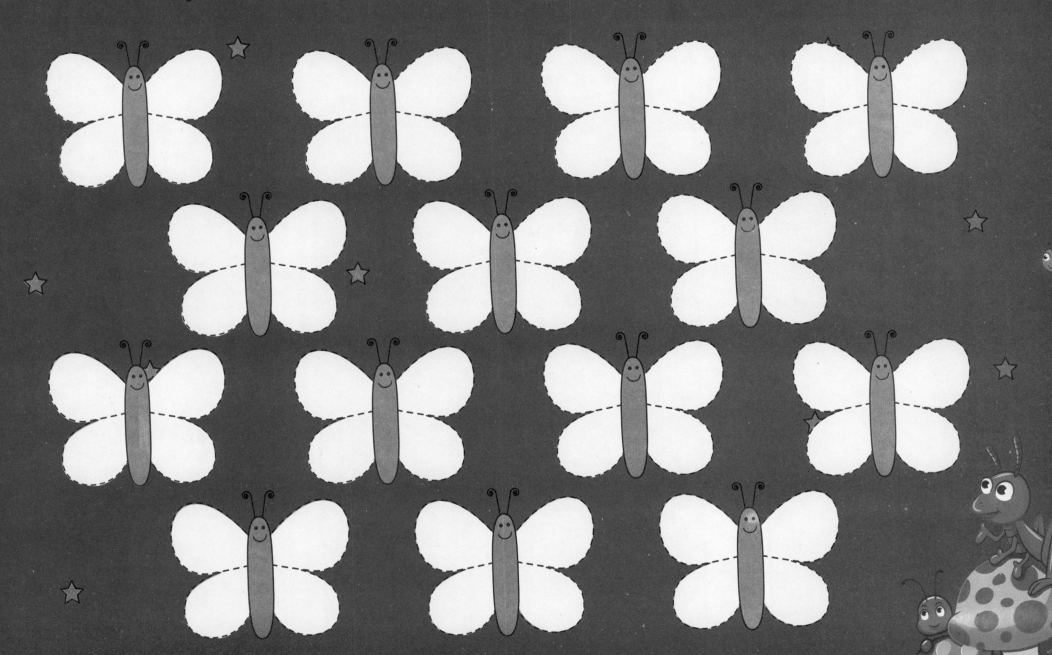

Bat Attack

Trace the lines to draw bats. Color the bats brightly.

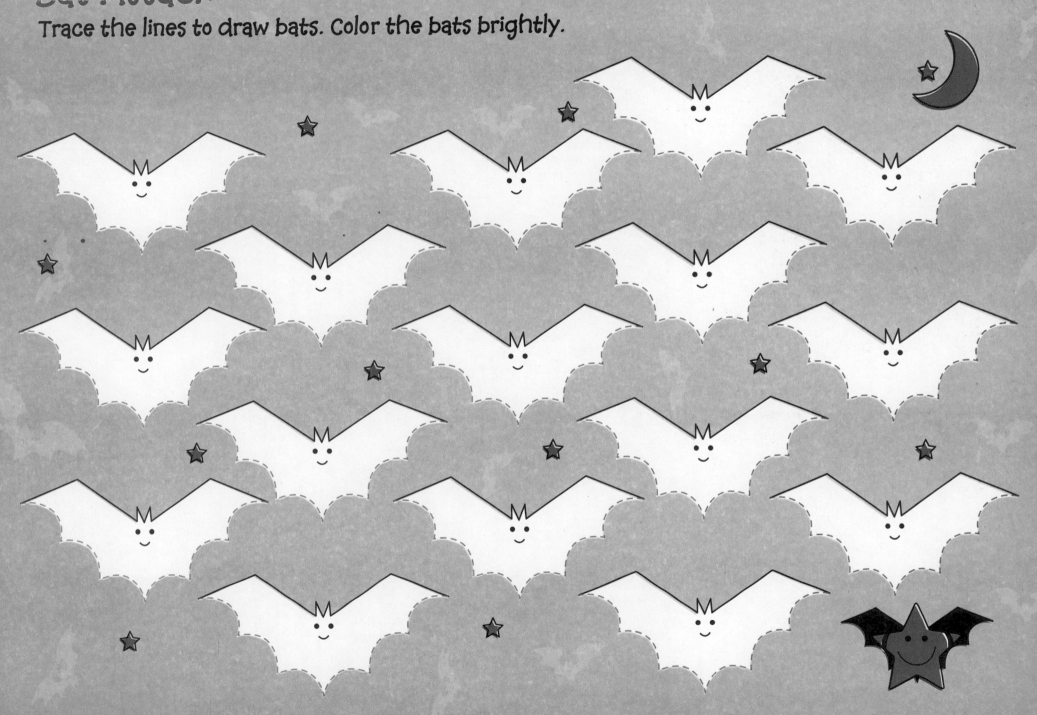

Coconut Grove

Trace the lines and draw the coconut trees.
Color the trees brightly.

Caterpillar Food

Trace the patterns to draw the caterpillars. Color the caterpillars brightly.

Sheep Farm

Trace the lines to draw the sheep grazing in the farm.

Midnight Swim

Trace the lines to complete the artwork.

start

start

Marine Life

Trace the lines to draw the fish. Color the fish brightly.

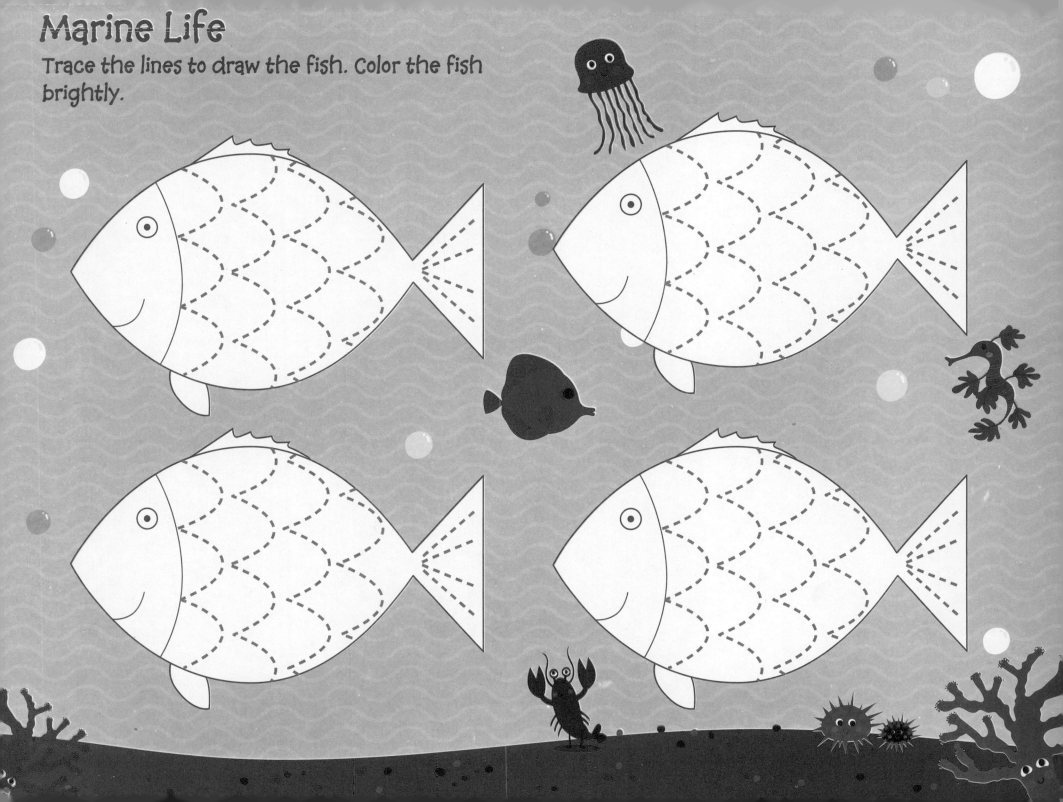

Heroic Firemen

Help the firemen find the right path to the burning building.

UNDER CONSTRUCTION

SHOP